# A JOURNEY TO REMEMBER

## BY

## Ada T. Mattox

-- Sketch designed by Martha McMullan

*From the Author – Ada Mattox*
*Decades ago a teacher gave me an A+ on a theme I had written. Below was a comment, "You have a great gift!" From that point on, I have felt the daily compulsion to apply pen to every paper available*

*Through the years many friends have suggested that I publish my poems, but it was my former pastor, the Rev. J. Glenn Linthicum, who put feet to my dream and did all the work necessary to finally make this book possible.*

*Writing is my therapy. My prayer is that something in this collection may speak to your heart also.*

A Journey to Remember

Cover Design by Cover Designer

Printed in the United States of America

First Printing: November 6. 2018

ISBN-9781729214978

# CONTENTS

# FOREWORD

In her collection of poems, Ada Mattox proclaims that she has had a lifelong love for words, and her poems reveal her penchant for rhyme as she takes the reader on her journey the way a guide for whitewater rafters steers riders from a calm beginning through turbulent rapids back to the tranquility of still water near the journey's end. Near the beginning of her collection she writes in "Words," "I have had a love affair with words."

Her love affair with words propels her to pave the road of her journey with rhyme. Along her journey she shares her frustration in a poem by that name by writing about her muse, "For eighteen years she sang in my ear/When I was much too busy to hear /I had diapers to fold and babies to hold/Meals in the making that must not get cold."

Throughout her collection she reaffirms her faith in God despite the challenges and disappointments she faces, including coping with the loss of loved ones and life changing events. In "Quest for Beauty" she praises God, "Thank you, God, for letting me see/Majesty in each towering tree. /When I shall sit at Jesus's feet, /My quest for beauty will be complete."

Sharing in "Our Hectic Household" what parenting four children is like while serving as a minister's wife, she provides insight, "The house underwent some transformation:/The Indianapolis Speedway, Grand Central Station. /The drums, piano, and saxophone/Yielded only to the telephone."

In a confessional poem entitled "Old Habits," the poet "comes to grip" with the loss of her husband who pastored a church for many years, "I have learned many things in your absence:/To be alone without crying, /To bake one potato instead of two, /To open my own doors, /To call repairmen when something breaks, /And how to pump gas at the service station."

One of her most poignant poems reveals her reaction to the death of her son. In "My Joel" she renders, "If that is my Joel lying there in death, /At least he no longer struggles for breath. /Pain cannot touch him now; he's with God at last/Where I shall join him when this life has passed."

As she confronts her own mortality, she admits that she is nearing her journey's end. In "Betrayal," she writes, "My body now betrays me, /Refuses to do my will;/It will not stay awake all day/Or climb a rocky hill."

Reflecting on her realization that her physical limitations are increasing, "In Growing Old," the poet confesses, "My body shrinks; I'm not as tall. /My greatest fear is that I will fall. /Energy leaves; it doesn't last. /Working all day is a thing of the past."

In "Life in Assisted Living," she reminds the reader that aging has its own challenges, "Now my days stretch out before me;/My daily planner is put away. /Nothing is scribbled under the heading, /Things that I must do today."

Near the end of her collection, "Withdrawing Deposits" reveals her need for motivation to continue her physical struggle, "Each fall I long to go to school;/Daily I miss my church as I pray./These memories have become a needed tool/To make my body want to start the day."

In **A Journey to Remember**, the poet shares her personal experiences as a minister's wife who struggles to cope with parenting four children. Ultimately, she shares with her readers her pain of losing loved ones, her frustration with coping with problems while living as a widow, and her physical struggle with the debilitating effects of diabetes and aging. Rather than any muse, it is evident that God has inspired Ada Mattox to share her life's journey.

Ray Allen, friend and fellow poet

Mr. Ray Allen made his debut as a poet in 1968 as a featured reader at the opening ceremony of the Douglas House Center in Long Beach, California. During the past 50 years, Allen has won numerous poetry awards, and in 1991 Morehead State University's Alumni Association inducted him as its 80th member. With four books of poetry to his credit and two songs that have been recorded, he continues to write poetry and songs. In 2006 Encyclopedia of Appalachia, a publication by the University of Tennessee Press, featured Allen as a post-World War poet.

# EASY INDEX

# Part #3: *My Guide*

# Part #4: *My Fellow Travelers*

## Part #5: *Wayside Reflections*

## Part #6: *The Passing Seasons*

# Part #7: *Special Days*

# Part #8: *Near Journey's End*

# THE JOURNEY BEGINS

## Lost Poetic Lines

At the beginning of the day,
Words so quickly come my way,
"Soon I'll write them down," I say,
But the muse declines to stay.

How I wish that I could find
All those lines that cross my mind
Until I could quickly find
Pen and paper of some kind.

Initial words are always best.
After that begins a quest
To capture that original zest,
But nothing else can pass the test.

Sometimes I think I'm on the verge
Of having these lost lines emerge
In one overwhelming surge
Before I lose the urge.

But in reality, today
I must admit that, come what may,
With the fisherman I must say,
"Those are the ones that got away."

# *Words*

I have had a lifelong love of words.
From the time I first read about Baby Ray
Until the morning news I read today,
I have had a love affair with words.

Just as a jeweler selects a stone
That creates the lasting beauty he intends,
So writers must select the word that lends
Enhancement to a before-established tone.

This world holds many idols to embrace:
Movie stars, athletes, heads of state,
But the ones who with genius I equate
Are those who put proper words in place.

Beauty surrounds us everywhere we gaze:
Day's end with sunset and evening star,
Oceans and mountains and valleys flung far.
Words that describe them never cease to amaze.

## Creative Urgency

In my cocoon I have missed the springtime;
This erstwhile butterfly failed to emerge.
Somehow, I fell short of achievement;
I linger here, just on the verge.

Help me break through the walls that encase me;
My folded wings long to fly.
Help me fulfill the promise this season,
Lest the urge die.

## Frustration

My muse will not be hurried.
For eighteen years she sang in my ear
When I was much too busy to hear.
I had diapers to fold and babies to hold,
Meals in the making that must not get cold—
Now, I'm getting worried.
Is her voice now to be still
When I have volumes of pages to fill?
With time on my hands and fewer demands
And the need to express myself expands,
Can her favor not be curried?

# *Well-Chosen Words*

With a pocket full of freshly-minted words,
I set out to redescribe my world.
Into fountains bright I tossed them,
Invested them in minds of eager children,
Divided them with others working outside the box.
Reveled in the ecstasy of shared wonder.

# *ALONG THE PATHWAY*

## *First Light*

Before my window I receive a new day
    from God's hand.
In prayer I watch while sunshine spreads
    across the verdant land.
Beyond the velvety grassy field,
    dense trees lift branches high
And lift the curtains open on a
    flawless, cloudless sky.

Another way God shows His boundless
    care is this:
That I can feel in nature this fulfilling bliss.
He fills my cup of wonder in endless
    kinds of ways.
And brings new inspiration to
    a string of tasteless days.

I cannot even imagine a look
    at Eden's scene
When the world and everything in it was
    new and fresh and clean.
When God walked with man and shared
    how everything should be.
But today a little glimpse of Eden
    I am blessed to see.

# *My Silent Sentinel*

Outside my window you stand guard in every
    season.
Billows of green, by many considered to be more
    lovely,
In summer encase your towering skeleton.
Coy breezes teasingly lift your skirts
Until the brazen autumn gales
Strip you of your finery.

Pencil-thin limbs in intricate tracery
Brace themselves against a leaden sky,
Allowing my spirit space to breathe
Beneath this loathsome winter.
Soon spring will revive my awesome sentinel,
Filling in the intervals with a welcome green.
Emerging leaflets will invite the warming wind
To lift and dance among their swirling petticoats.

I have observed your cycle, my constant sentinel,
As you have watched mine.
In the end, when all facades
And conventions of society fall away,
Beauty will be revealed in your gnarled constancy
And unaltered will to persevere.

# Quest for Beauty

From somewhere in my distant past,
Into my mind today there flashed
An image of a flower bed
Completely filled with blossoms red.

My life has been long and complete
Filled to the brim with memories sweet:
The adoring looks of loving faces,
Visions of God's created spaces.

Oh, I have truly loved this earth,
The treasured country of my birth:
The balmy breeze, the sunset's glow,
Fields of daisies, row on row.

Thank you, God, for letting me see
Majesty in each towering tree.
When I shall sit at Jesus' feet,
My quest for beauty will be complete,

## *God's Greatness*

Each day at dusk, I scan the forest's edge
And search again at dawn,
Hoping to see a graceful deer--
A mighty buck, a graceful doe, a gentle fawn.

Spindly legs that seem so frail
Are poised for instant flight.
Nostrils that flare and eyes that dart
Speak of constant fright.

The flighty nature of the deer
In humans is shared by each.
Until our faith in God matures,
Contentment lurks just out of reach.

Forgive me the times I doubt Your love
And think the outcome depends on me.
When I can release the reins to You,
How much smoother life will be.

Uncertainties, anxieties, doubts, and fears
Could rob my life of all that's good.
Help me banish those negative thoughts
And follow You as I know I should.

# Nocturnal Display

I awaken to booms of thunder;
Lightning flashes stab the night.
To polish off this show of wonder,
A driving rain obscures the light.

I used to fear the summer storm
And quickly closed the blinds or drape
When I saw a dark cloud form;
Now I watch with mouth agape.

Once I stood on an ocean beach
And watched angry waves come crashing in.
I managed to stay just out of their reach
By moving backward again and again.

A part of me wants white clouds and soft breezes
That give me the feeling that everything's well.
But nature-gone-mad my other side pleases
When forces long dormant begin to rebel.

When life is filled with routine days,
Existence becomes unbearably dull;
But when chaos makes my life a maze,
I long for a much-needed lull.

God makes us creatures familiar with change.
As we journey together down life's highway,
He allows us emotions that broadly range
So that no day is like any other day.

## *The Big Wind*

The day was almost gone when the wind began to blow;
It clawed hungrily at my door and bent my trees.
As its intensity increased, my fear began to grow
For this was certainly no ordinary breeze.

A nearby transformer boomed; darkness filled the room.
To pass the hours ahead, what would I do?
I surely could not read in this deepening gloom;
My activity options seemed so very few.

There will be no heat; food may spoil in the frig.
I cannot cook, enjoy TV, or wash my clothes.
The water pipes may freeze—I don't want to cross
    that bridge--
 For I have seen the damage that can quickly come
    from those.

I do not like this wind that leaves havoc in its wake;
And I detest the inconvenience in my day.
But when I named the routes in darkness I could take,
I left out the most constructive: I could pray.


## Day's End

The blazing sun set fires across the sky;
A far-off bell announced the end of day.
I watched a lone hawk rise nearby and fly
To catch and hold a quickly dying ray.

# MY GUIDE

## Live Life Fully

"Meaningless" is a word I hate to hear.
It falls with certain sadness on my ear.
It speaks of dull and repetitious acts,
Of life reduced to cold, distasteful facts.

I want to relish each day to the full,
Escape the humdrum, the downward pull,
Make my life here a joyous parade,
Resist all that would cause purpose to fade.

Each year should be measured by what I have done,
A journal reflecting a race well-run.
Time here on earth is a priceless gift--
Not intended to be spent in a careless drift.

Life is much better when God walks beside,
When I submit and let Him be my guide.
Troubles still surround me, and pain will not end,
But my days have meaning, for God is my friend.

# *Enduring With Joy*

Joyfully follow to the very end
Life's road that can change at every bend.
Today may be cheerless, empty, and bare;
Tomorrow may be sunny with merriment to spare.

When life's burdens compound and become too much,
I long for God's presence and His healing touch.
Disappointment and heartaches exact a great toll,
But God's spirit can refresh my downtrodden soul.

Where would I be without my best friend?
Nobody but God can my broken heart mend.
He is my light in the tunnel ahead;
By Him my faltering spirit is fed.

Some days I feel I just can't go on,
Every ounce of my strength completely gone.
Then I remember I'm not in control;
I've made God the master of my soul.

# Recognition

God, in the early morning hour I adore You;
To Your canon and Your precepts I am true.
But I must sincerely say,
If I'm to make it through the day,
I am going to need a lot of help from You.

## *My Lord*

Wearily I lean upon You;
From my cares I am set free.
Lord and Master, I adore You.
You are everything to me.

# Redemption

I would drink of Your spirit;
I would grow in Your grace.
I would lift up my neighbor;
I would show him Your face.

All my sins are forgiven
You have covered each one.
My redemption was purchased
By Your own blessed Son.

# Discovery

I bend my will to Yours.
So intent was I on finding a way
I did not know for--oh, so long--
My purpose countermanded Yours.

I have loved You, Lord, all my life
(The part I remember anyway),
But every day I discover things about You
That I never even thought or knew before.

# MY FELLOW TRAVELERS

## My Two Fathers

My earthly father was a man of toil.
From break of dawn until the dark of night,
He tilled the sometimes barren, rocky soil,
Planted crops, and reaped when the time was right.

The Great Depression slowly choked our land;
We felt the profound bitterness of need.
You would have had to live then to understand
The stress he felt with eight mouths to feed.

He wore old overalls and a broad-brimmed hat.
The denim felt rough when he held me on his knee
As he read to me from Shakespeare—imagine that.
He was my daddy, and he meant the world to me.

I heard I had a Heavenly Father too
Who made the world and all that in it is.
He promised to give life anew
To all who would surrender and be His.

When I was twelve, I was able to decide
To find joy in Him rather than be forever sad.
Two days later my earthly father died;
Then God was the only Father that I had.

# Saving for Old Age

My mother saved carefully for her old age:
Bits of twine and paper bags sequestered in dark
   drawers,
Remnants of thread that had sewed our childhood
   dresses,
Buttons that displayed nearly a century of fashion.
These important things she intentionally saved.

She knew nothing of jewelry or stocks and bonds
That people traditionally stash,
Her hands now idle for want of something else to do
Scrubbed clothes outdoors in a tub over a fire,
Cracked open as she milked cows in predawn hours.
Wrung substance from depression circumstances.

She always saved that one good dress,
For nobody knew when an occasion might arise
When she would need that very thing to wear
Along with a pair of stockings that had no runs.
There might be a wedding or a funeral.
She has also saved thinking about death until old age.
At ninety-two she now concedes that it might come,
But she has saved it for her very old age.

# The Vigil

The breath goes in;
The breath goes out,
And life goes on
All about.

Outside the room
A small bird sings,
Tree leaves rustle,
A church bell rings.

Upon that bed
My mother lies,
And slowly, sadly now
She dies.

Nothing else matters,
Nothing at all,
But watching her bosom
Rise and fall.

# My Minister Husband

As a bride, I starched and ironed his shirts
With adoration.
He was a vision, aloof and elevated upon
A public pedestal.
Our people loved him too, and they would say,
"He was such a comfort to us when Papa died."

We have faced a lot together now, we two.
Four children and four churches later, I hate to iron.
The pedestal is lower now, but I have learned what
People meant when they said:
"He was such comfort to us when Papa died."

# *Aftermath*

They all came to mourn his passing:
Brothers and sister,
Children and grandchildren.
They came to contemplate the empty space
He left in all their lives.

The widow sat with swollen eyelids
Trying hard to keep her composure in public.

They have all gone home now
To lives not built upon his daily presence.
The tears will dry, and they will be ashamed
Of how well they have adjusted to living without him.

The widow returns to surroundings that speak
Of over forty years of shared existence.
Before nightfall she will think of a dozen things
She wishes she could tell him.

# Old Habits

It is half-past five, the appointed time for
   your daily return home,
I strain to hear the car pull into the driveway,
The slamming of the car door,
The key turning in the lock,
Your announcement: "Hello, I'm home."
But all I hear is silence.

It has been this way for a long time now--
Through years following your early retirement,
Your struggle to adjust,
Your search for new meaning in life,
A long and cruel illness,
Your leave-taking that May evening
When you called out to God, "Hello, I'm home."
Did you ask what was for dinner?

I have learned many things in your absence:
To be alone without crying,
To bake one potato instead of two,
To open my own doors,
To call repairmen when something breaks,
And how to pump gas at the service station.
Someday, perhaps, I will learn that
No one comes at half-past five.

# *Your Presence*

As I squint my eyes against the sun,
A shadow falls across my face.
Is it you from beyond that doorway we call death,
Still protecting and caring for me?
It is so much like you to do that.

As I lie alone in the bed we shared,
I feel your shoulder cradling my head.
Is this some dream that taunts me in my lonely hours,
Or is it you comforting and holding me?
You promised you would never leave me.

As I walk alone the pathway we once took together,
I feel someone walking close beside me.
If you are there, why can't you hold my hand
And laugh the way we used to do?
No, it is enough for me to feel that you are near.

## *Our Hectic Household*

Where is the peace and quiet we knew
When there were only just we two?
Under the stereo's brassy blare?
Under the hoofbeat on the stair?

Perhaps it fled that very day
We asked that little blond to stay.
He gathered in a host of others:
Neighbors, school friends, sister, brothers.

When the infant cry dismissed the night,
His older siblings arose to fight
"She kicked my shins." "He used my brush!"
"Won't you simply eat and hush?"

Revolution grew into wars full blown
For possession of the bathroom throne.
Among treasured memories that is right
Next to my favorite, "Friends over night."

The house underwent some transformation:
The Indianapolis Speedway, Grand Central Station.
The drum, piano, and saxophone
Yielded only to the telephone.

But the day will shortly be
When we will again be two or three,
And I will long to hear once more
The awful din of children four.

## *Another Day*

Lord, it can't be time to rise.
Must I open wide my eyes
In this home that's partly nursery, partly zoo?
Now I confidently say:
If I'm to make it through the day
That I'm going to need a lot of help from You.

The dogs scratch at the door
And they puddle on the floor
If I'm not quick enough to honor their request.
The cats demand to eat,
And they rub around my feet;
Water, dry food, wet food—all must pass their test.

Now the baby must be fed,
After lifting her from her bed.
Her piercing screams can hardly be ignored,
I can't say, "Wait your turn,

It's a lesson you must learn."
To a little one unquestionably adored.

While they irritate and stress
And create a constant mess,
They enrich my life and make it more complete.
One toothless baby grin
Is enough my heart to win.
The devotion of my pets is hard to beat.


## *Promise*

My daughter stands with woman's grace,
A hint of beauty in her face.
Thoughts are feelings she must ponder.
Time is an element to squander;

Days pass through a sieve so small
That they seem not to pass at all.
Do you think she will discover
All the many ways I love her?

# Fair Trade

When she was three, she used to say,
"If you don't let me go to Naomi's,
I'll say my three bad words!"

They weren't really bad--
Just bathroom talk her school-age brothers
Had generously shared--
But embarrassing in front of little old ladies
And proper gentlemen.

Now, at twelve, in a hurtful mood she shouts,
"I hate you!"
If it were all the same with her,
I would rather hear her three bad words.

# With My Daughter in Church

I feel the merriment well up
Like sparkling bubbles in a cup.
Soon our gales of stifled laughter
Shake the pews before and after.
Cherubim desert their perch
When I sit with her in church.

# Going Away to College

Our comfortable pattern of life is changing.
For the last eighteen years
We have tracked the selfsame star in neighboring
orbits –
Seldom close enough to crowd or stifle
But near enough for security and warmth.
That comfortable pattern is to be no more.

Now the sweeping magnet of God's love
Has drawn our lives into a different realm.
No longer will I share with you the daily path
Or know the reassurance of your touch.
Knowing that distant stars cry out to you,
I am resigned, at last, to see you go.

My prayer for you is not for calm and easy days.
The joy that comes to you may follow pain.
Only know the inner peace that God may give
To those who know and do His perfect will.
He will watch between us through the years
Until He holds us both together in His arms.

## Switching Places

Could you not see the furrows in my brow,
You would not treasure the smoothness of your skin.
If I did not your foolishness disdain,
I might pine for tender youth again.

## Revolt

I cannot mother
    Another
This little brood of four
    Is more
Than I can cover.

## Out of Pocket

Born to run free in open meadows
Where the dazzling sun bathes your golden hair
And turns your skin to bronze,
I have confined you to four walls and city streets.

Be patient yet awhile
Until time shall ease that longing to be free,
And you shall learn at last to live
Within fences of your own building.

## Rush of Wonder

My four-year-old tugged at my hand and my heart.
Come, Mommy, let me show you something,
Something truly remarkable!

My heart overflowed with love and wonder.
You, my son,
You are something truly remarkable!

# Twice Chosen

"They picked me! They picked me!"
Oh, the depth of his pride!
The sweetness of belonging
Was too much to hide.
"We picked you! We picked you!"
I thought as I kissed him.
How ordinary life would have been
If we'd missed him.

# *Surprise!*

"Look mom! I made it myself!"
This surprise cannot be hidden behind him
Like the papers he brings with colorful squiggles.
It is a coat rack he made in shop.

Love doesn't make me blind exactly;
It just makes me indiscriminate.
I see the places where the stain has puddled.
Like wormholes in fine wood, they make it more
   valuable.

# My Joel

That's not my son lying there so still.
He's somewhere running on a sun-dappled hill,
Or in a dense woodland hunting deer,
Or down by the river with his fishing gear.

That's not my son with folded hands.
He's playing a drum, beating rhythm with bands.
Tinkering with cars or applying wax,
Polishing to restore the luster it lacks.

No, my son is eager to get his fill
Of the chicken roasting on the backyard grill.
He's planting a garden or playing with the dog,
Riding a Harley or splitting a log.

He's saying he loves me and all others:
Wife and children and sister and brothers,
His friends he has cherished through all these years,
Those who have shared his laughter and tears.

If that is my Joel lying there in death,
At least he no longer struggles for breath.
Pain cannot touch him now; he's with God at last
Where I shall join him when this life is past.

## Losing a Child

There are many ways to lose a child;
Death is only one.
Mental illness claimed my daughter,
And distance took my son.

## Finding Comfort

He pounces on me in the night=-
My no-tail cat with eyes so bright.
He nestles into the covers deep;
Then both of us fall fast asleep.
We each to the other a gift imparts:
I warm his body; he warms my heart.

I cast myself on God above
And seek the comfort of His love.
He shoulders the burdens that I bear
And reassures me of His care.
What greater relationship could there be?
For I love Him, and He loves me.

## *College Reunion Reflections*

The years have dealt gently with us.
Sifting with a generous hand,
They have gifted us with
Mates and children,
Careers and influence,
Dreams and realities
That reach far beyond the walls that framed us.

Floods and fortune have drawn us into alien
    confluences.
There we mixed our heritage of depression years,
A nation united by war, and
Post War prosperity
With the world of our progeny,
Fast paced and dissonant.

But we have nourished the flame set
Aglow in us by our mentors.
Together still we stand,
United by purpose,
Impassioned by knowledge,
True to our fellow comrades,
Passing to succeeding generations the torch entrusted.

When we were young,
We drew each from the other
The sustaining nutrients of life:
Love and affirmation,
Companionship and concern,
A sense of belonging and worth.
We became in the process more than
    A sum of our parts.

Years later when we meet,
Hiding within us who we were
But revealing who we have become:
Encouragers of the young,
Builders of a better future,
Connected friends.
Those depositing their lives in our
Account are validated.

# *Nothing Lasts*

It is the time of year for leaves to fall:
The wild geese call.
We know full well from seasons past
Things cannot last.

A special one we hoped would stay,
Has gone away.
His place is empty now and bare;
He is not there.

But One who knows our every need
Is near indeed.
And friends who understand and care
Our sorrows share.

# WAYSIDE REFLECTIONS

## *Guilt*

Was it only yesterday
When I bowed my head to pray,
That the words came quickly tumbling to my mind?
Syllables of honor, gladness, praise,
All the love my heart could raise
To my God who is so merciful and kind.

Today the world seems dark and drear,
And I strain my ears to hear
The reassurance that I crave from You.
Harsh words that I have said
Keep running through my head.
Give me strength to do as You would have me do.

## *Better Words*

There ought to be a better way to say, "Thank you"
To the One who died for me,
To the One who set me free--
Different from what I tell my dear friend Sue
When she brings a lovely gift
Or provides a needed lift.

There ought to be another way to say "I love you"
To the One who intercedes
And who meets my deepest needs--
Different from what I tell my closest few
Who walk with me through life's maze
And bring joy to darkest days.

Until I find there is a better way,
I will repeat these same old phrases when I pray.

# Sense of Duty

A sense of duty is a compelling thing.
It makes me vacuum the dusty floors
When I would rather be on the porch swing,
Enjoying the refreshing out-of-doors.  ·

My Christian duty forbids me to hate;
Instead of that, I must forgive.
I can't even wish a terrible fate
If I'm to live as God wants me to live.

Duty breaks the shackles of sleep
And banishes my comfy cocoon.
It whispers of promises I must keep
If my life is to be played in tune.

Think of where this world will be
If nobody answers when duty calls;
We will no longer be safe or free
Without people to help when disaster befalls.

# *I Wonder*

Some strange questions cross my mind:
Were Mary and Joseph always kind?
Did Mary have post-partum depression?
Did Joseph worry about a recession?
Did Mary have a constant battle
Keeping Jesus away from the cattle?

Then these other thoughts ensue:
In Jesus' spare time, what did He do?
When did He first drink from a cup?
Who was His best friend growing up?
Did his young siblings resent big brother?
How much background was shared by mother?

What was His favorite thing to eat?
Did He get blisters on His feet?
What place on earth did He like best?
What made that different from the rest?

As His humanity I explore,
It only makes me love Him more.

## Good Days Remembered

Thank you, God, for days like this
That fly on silvery wings.
When everything falls into place
Before the doorbell rings.

## Troubles

They settle in like the dark of night,
Obscuring all that's joyful and bright.
They squeeze relentlessly around my heart
And tear my comfortable world apart.

Sometimes they wage a sneak attack
And slip upon me from my back;
At other times I watch them near,
And I am paralyzed with fear.

The little ones are not too bad,
But even they will make me sad.
The big ones turn my life around
And leave me lying upside down.

I try so hard as I make my way
Through the turbulence of everyday
To scatter peace and calm about
As I shut negativity and bickering out.

# *Undecided*

Some people philosophize just like that
At the snap of a finger, the drop of a hat.
They know what they think, and they're happy to tell
    it.
There's one idea to buy, and they alone sell it.

I find myself wavering, considering, deciding,
Avoiding the absolute, dogmatism deriding,
Seeing the good points of one side then the other,
Forsaking one thought and grasping another.

There are a lot of things in life to know–
Besides if beans should be cooked fast or slow.
How to rear a child from birth to youth
Is a lifetime challenge, not a moment of truth.

I wish I had the gift to know
How to do and where to go.
Maybe...

# Slave Labor

There is a high cost in loving.

There is the toil of menial labor
Nobody could hire you to do.

There are the fears that build mischievous boys
     into bank robbers
And simple viruses into fatal diseases.

There is the frustration of pulling onto your
     own shoulders
The accumulated burdens of everyone you know.

There is the strain of trying to be everything
     to everyone
Until you feel you are nothing to anyone.

You have to budget your emotions to afford love.

# Youth

If this is what youth is like,
Then I was never young.
I didn't put dishes under my bed
Or leave my clothes unhung.
I went to bed when it was dark
And got up when it was day;
I had the idea that I must work
Before I had time to play.

I've found that cooking meals at home
Is not how to have food.
I can simply order and have it prepared
If I'm not in the cooking mood.
A phone was something that hung on the wall
That now and then would ring.
I didn't have Twitter and Facebook and such
With all the drama they bring.

Holes in clothes and patches sewn on
Were the epitome of poverty's shame.
I took responsibility when I erred;
I didn't know parents were to blame.
Somehow, I missed that the seamy side
Was something to be explored,
While the Savior who died on the cross for us
Was sadly, completely ignored.

# Improbable

Improbable --
That she who placed the golden circlet on his
    finger,
Its worth to him more than gold could ever buy,
Could find it in the bottom of the river
Forever lost, it seemed, from human eye.
But she did!

Improbable.


# My Country

This is not the country in which I grew up.
The illusions of my childhood are all shattered.
The battle cries of heroes that fired my youthful
    imagination
Seem empty now--pathetic prologue unrelated
To a turbulent present.

# Coping

I have learned to cope with life's unusual ways
    On sunny days,
But when dark clouds keep scurrying by,
    Sometimes I cry.

# Catharsis

Dark smoke rises from my chimney,
Snaking its way into the upper air
Where it thins into a soft gray mist.
Such is sorrow.

Convulsive spasms of despair and hopelessness
Constrict and paralyze my human spirit
Until they are released in frantic sobs.
What will it matter a hundred years from now
That the fire turned into ashes that last oak log
While I, too, longed to be reduced to nothingness?

# Restorers of Light

He stood before me, gazing into my eyes.
His object was not romance;
He didn't want to dance.
"I clearly see wherein your problem lies.
It's a cataract,
To be exact."

"If left to grow, it could block out the light.
Not to be unkind,
But you could go blind.
A simple surgery will restore your sight;
How much better life will be
If you can see!"

My Heavenly Father looks into my eyes.
I am a child He bought;
He knows my every thought.
He sees wherein my spiritual problem lies;
"If you are to grow,
This sin must go."

As I trusted the surgeon to restore my physical sight,
I trust my God to give me spiritual light.

# Post Mastectomy

An ugly scar bisects my chest
Where once there was a woman's breast.
Inside I rant and seethe with rage;
A lioness stalks within this cage.
It isn't fair!
But I must not care.

A wild cell lurks just out of view,
Content to wait a year or two
Until it finishes its task.
(Each time it wears a different mask.)
I'm going to die,
But I must not cry.

Now who will hear my small son's wail,
Adjust my daughter's wedding veil?
And what of him whose hand I hold
More tightly as the days grow cold?
How strange to think that he will be
No longer another part of me.
I love him so.
Why must I go?

My aging mother bids me stay
The debt of childhood to repay
She laid her second-born to rest
In many ways she loved her best.
Her eyesight wanes.
Aloneness pains.

I know that I was born to die,
But the sun is still so high.
The image I would sharply etch
Is but a faintly outlined sketch.
How swift the flight to that "Goodnight!"

# THE PASSING SEASONS

## The Passing Seasons

Let the wheel go around again;
Each turn brings much of joy and pain.
The crocus blossoms at my feet;
Then comes the blinding summer heat
And the breathless hush of fall
Before the snow that covers all.
Some days bring sunshine; some bring rain.
Let the wheel go around again.

In the mirror I see my face.
The ceaseless seasons left their trace.
The child I was, I cannot see.
No mark of youth is left in me.
Determination still is there,
A ready smile, some sparks of fire.
My faith in God will keep me sane;
Let the wheel go around again.

# *February*

February, how she teases,
Doing exactly as she pleases!
Instead of bringing tons of snow,
Flowers bloom and tree leaves grow.

I know some people just like that,
Who daily don a different hat.
Just when you have them figured out,
They do a perplexing turnabout.

God alone is ever the same;
He doesn't play the "Sometimes" game.
When I trust Him day by day,
I know He's with me all the way.

I sometimes rue the way things go
And do not like to suffer so,
But if He who holds the master plan
Thinks I can manage, then I can.

# *March*

As March approaches, I long to see
New foliage appearing on each lofty tree,
Daffodils making their cheery display,
Kites flying above fields across the way.

I am eager to feel soft winds embrace
My smiling, upturned waiting face,
As the sun lures lilies out of the ground
Each place a sleeping bulb is found.

I pull the grill out of the shed,
Put line-dried sheets on every bed,
Store heavy woolens and locate the green,
For soon St. Patrick will be making the scene.

How good is God who can make hearts sing
With all rapture this season can bring.
I welcome March with open arms,
Grateful for the way my life it warms.

# *April*

April, shivering still with cold,
Brought all the joy my heart could hold,
Dotted hills with lambs and flowers,
Washed them fresh in springtime showers.

There is so much in life I treasure
That I find it hard to measure
What in nature moves me more
As this season I explore.

Soft dawns await my waking eyes
With pools of sunlight and azure skies.
Male cardinals with their brilliant red
Coax the sleepy one out of bed.

Oh, I have known so many springs.
As each one special splendor brings,
I humbly thank my Father above
For creating so much for me to love.

# *May*

May untied my apron strings
And turned me out to play.
The dusty floors, the dirty clothes
Could wait one other day.

She led me by a babbling brook
And made my heart feel glad
To see a tiny, peeping frog
Upon a lily pad.

The grass felt soft beneath my feet
While sunshine warmed my back.
I sat beneath a poplar tree
And raided my lunch sack.

Dandelions embraced my feet
And brightened up my day.
A hymn of praise burst from my lips
And I began to pray.

# School in Springtime

The weary year draws to a close;
A soft breeze blows.
The roses sing of days long past
That did not last.

I find time flows more quickly now;
Don't ask me how.
Each moment owns its share of gold
I try to hold.

The children dream of summer days
Seen through a haze;
Their facts and figures they forgot
As the sun turned hot.

# Summer

Wrest from spring her store of laughter;
Pull the breathless calm from fall.
Bind them back to back with sunshine;
Add a raucous blue jay's call.

Cardinals blaze a path of splendor;
Sunflowers lift their faces high.

Puffy clouds like cotton candy
Drift across a pale, blue sky.

Soft breezes ease the heat of noontime,
Bringing memories of the past:
Games of hopscotch and red rover,
Youthful dreams we thought would last

Backyard grills entice us homeward
Offering ribs with spicy sauce.
Adults linger around the table
While kids enjoy a game of toss.

Golden days stretch out before us;
Oceans call us to their shores.
Friends and family come to visit;
Summer opens many doors.

## Summer Day

The sinking sun laid sleepy velvet shadows
In ever-changing patterns at my door.
Sounds and time were muted, then suspended;
Contentment flowed like liquid from each pore.


## The March of Time

The sweltering summer slipped away
With sound of mower, scent of hay.
Oh, how I tried to make her stay
This is my catch-up season.

The autumn morn is crisp and cool,
And I am once again in school.
The hourglass I cannot fool
Whatever be the reason.

# Autumn's Web

My labored breathing slowed,
I could remember days when I had climbed that hill
With half the effort.
Never mind; it was enough to be here.

The sapling that I clutched
And pulled against my face was cool and rough.
My thickened palm felt comfort in its weathered bark.
"Two of a kind," I thought.

Sunlight snuggled warmly at my feet;
It came reluctantly to mosses unaccustomed to its
    presence.
The leaves that had long denied it access here
Had gone to rest.

Far away a lone bird cried;
The valleys stretched away in bands of empty silence.
The solitude of nature fed my soul,
And I was content.

Behind me, down the path that I had come,
Lay the city I call home.
It was quaint and picturesque from away up here
But often tiresome and dirty down below.

I lingered, caught in autumn's web,
Then turned with strong resolve to start the long way
    back.
When the sun went down, biscuits would be placed in
    the oven.
The habit of many years urged me not to be
    late.


## *Winter – Then and Now*

Winter was a joyous time when I was young;
I yearned to taste the snowflakes on my tongue.
A different cold now comes with sinister stealth
To challenge life and limb and warmth and health.

# SPECIAL DAYS

## A New Year

Given a fresh start, what shall we do:
Repeat our mistakes or write something new?
Break with the past as we resolve to do,
Or continue old behavior and not follow through?

This year can be different than those in the past;
We can build legacies that uplift and last,
Dedicate ourselves to a life lived for others,
Make all mankind like our sisters and brothers.

Let's weed out those habits that fill us with guilt,
Replace them with traits that are character-built.
Restore God to the place where He truly belongs,
And fill life with love and kindness and songs.

# A Valentine Recollection

Soft winds from long-forgotten springs
Brush by my mind on slivery wings;
The treasured touch, words gently spoken,
Love's first warm web, the promise unbroken.

The grin on your face declared your pride;
Love's prescription was not denied.
Chocolates and roses were quickly shared
Along with a card that said you cared.

The candlelight dinner wove its spell
As the magic of evening around us fell.
The years have erased much, but never this,
"My Valentine!" You whispered as you leaned
    down for a kiss.

# Celebration

You are advised:
You are recognized
For talent clearly undisguised.
It's celebration-sized;
Have yourself a celebration!

# *Easter – For Sinners Like Me*

Once I stood where it was said Jesus died,
On the skull-like hill where He was crucified.
And I thanked Him over and over again
For the blood He had spilled to cover my sin.
Unmatchable love!

I tried to picture the way He died:
The Roman spear that was thrust in His side,
The burdensome weight of the cross He bore,
The spikes that into His body tore.
Unimaginable pain!

But the pain of His body could not compare
With the anguish His Spirit had to bear.
Betrayal, rejection by those He held dear
While shouts born of hatred were all He could hear.
Heartbreaking trauma!

But when all seemed lost, great joy came,
And the world would never again be the same,
For out of this seeming tragedy,
He arose to rule for eternity.
Hallelujah! He lives!

## June Wedding

The languid summer lay in pools about the altar,
Tall candles flamed and swayed in careless dance,
Silken music wove a web of mystic memories,
The stage was ready then and marked "Romance."

The bride appeared to claim her knight in shining
  armor.
Her eagerness deplored the stately pace.
Her eyes were raised to his in adoration;
She paused to brush the dampness from his face.

## July

We welcome July
As we light up the sky
And proclaim the great worth
Of this land of our birth.

As the temperatures climb,
We often take time
For a refreshing iced tea
Or a trip to the sea.

Lazy evenings abound
As we relish the sound
Of cicadas and birds
And soft-spoken words.

Fireflies in a jar
And a strumming guitar
Form background for votes
For tall root beer floats.

Picnics in the park,
Campfires after dark,
Bike rides on trails,
Beside haystacks or bales

Reveal God up above
As he shows His great love
In His beautiful creation
And our freedom-blessed nation.

# *Thanksgiving Prayer*

For food and fun and loving friends
And all our Heavenly Father sends,
We give our thanks.

As we gather on this Thanksgiving Day,
In quietness we pause to pray
And give our thanks.

Accept the praise we raise today,
Hearing every word we say
As we give thanks.

# *Christmas Calm*

Christmas weaves its unique spells
Amid burning candles and ringing bells.
Hearts are warm although noses are cold;
Spirits are young even if bodies are old.
Carolers sing of the Savior's birth,
And men dare to dream of peace on earth.

We put up trees and colorful lights
That banish the darkness of the nights.
We shop and wrap the gifts we buy
And plan a menu with ham and pie.
Children seek out an unoccupied knee
And ask for stories with pictures to see.

Our hearts go out to those in need
As we bring bags of food the poor to feed.
Thoughts turn to home and those who are dear.
We travel great distances just to be near.
A hush seems to settle and bring a great calm
As Christmas arrives spreading beauty and balm.

# NEAR JOURNEY'S END

## Retort to Robert Browning

No, Mr. Browning, the latter stage of life is not the
    best!
It is not that I want do dance like I did at sixteen–
When Mother denied me that "sinful" pleasure,
But bending would be nice and stooping,
Being able to whip through my house,
Readying it for imminent visitors,
Walking again a fifteen-minute mile.

Old age, contrary to your rosy picture, sir,
Is anything but the best, especially on humid days.
Swollen ankles, creaking knees, a back
That painfully argues about an upright position
All file rebuttals to refute your romantic view.
While I used to dress to meet the day in ten minutes
    or so,
Now it takes me that long to button my shirt.

Inside this aging cage resides a somewhat
    active mind,
And--on most days--an untarnished, rust-proof
    spirit.
Was it for this painful stage that I rushed
    through life,
Wasting each day while I wished for
    a long string of tomorrows?
Not realizing that each hour held treasures
    now spent and forgotten?
Pushed now out of the main current
    into quiet eddies along the shore,
I find pleasure in little things like a leaf
    making circles in a sun-dappled pool.

# Coasting

I was a starship from my birth;
I blazed across uncharted skies,
There flamed a need to see it all,
To climb to where the last star lies.

The peak is reached, my fuel spent;
The wonder of my youth is past.
The upward surge is now a glide;
The distant stars in darkness cast.

I do not like this plodding pace;
The thrill of rising is no more.
The dreams I lost, I will not find.
How far to that distant shore?

# *Growing Old*

Aging brings its share of woes:
Memory is lost; the eyesight goes.
Arthritis travels down the spine.
Can that wrinkled face be mine?

My body shrinks; I'm not as tall.
My greatest fear is that I'll fall.
Energy leaves; it doesn't last.
Working all day is a part of my past.

The knees give out; it's hard to stand.
Hard, too, to grasp small things in my hand.
Once I longed to traipse everywhere.
Now I prefer to recline in my chair.

But one wonderful change has come with time,
A unique revelation so sublime:
I finally admit and cannot deny,
"I can do nothing; on God I rely."

## Being Upright

When I first prayed to be upright,
I was fighting sin with all my might,
Now that request again I send
Since gravity is not my friend.

## Our Changing Perspective

If our children left us as little tykes,
We would immediately rush to bring them back.
After enduring the frustrating teenage years,
We are almost ready to help them pack.

Leaving this world in the midst of life
Seems unthinkable, tragic, and sad
Until we experience the ravages of age.
Then departure doesn't seem so bad.

Our culture has made death complex,
With so much to do as it draws near;
More than the condition of being dead,
It is the process of dying that we fear.

Maybe we can just remain on earth
To hear that final trumpet blast.
Of all the experiences we have known
In life, this best would be the last.

## *My Daily Care*

It seems that I have landed on my feet:
Others cook the meals I eat,
Launder my clothes and shower me,
Put cream on my arthritic knee.

They keep my room neat as a pin,
Welcome all my friends and kin,
Invite in groups that dance and sing,
And others who Biblical messages bring.

Daily they stimulate our minds
With trivia, games, and word finds.
If all this does not our needs meet,
Movies and crafts are a frequent treat.

Meds are administered when they are due;
Every day brings adventure anew.
Bright halls are decked with holiday cheer
As each very special day draws near.

I am made to feel that I still have worth.
When I am sad, they interject mirth.
The treatment I get is a part of God's care
By people of compassion who are extremely rare.

Someone to help is always near;
Being alone is never a fear.
How grateful I am that I came to this place
Where I can find joy in each day I face.

# *Betrayal*

My body now betrays me,
Refuses to do my will;
It will not stay awake all day
Or climb a rocky hill.

It will no longer find the files
That hold memories of my past.
Once in a while a light bulb burns,
But the image doesn't last.

It creaks and groans as I move about
And fills my life with pains.
Arthritis dictates what I can do,
Especially when it rains.

But God has been more than good to me;
He hears my every prayer.
When I can no longer manage here,
I'll be with Him up there.

# Life in Assisted Living

Once my life was so demanding:
A house, a family, a career to pursue.
There was never enough time to finish
All the chores that I should do.

I took care of aging parents,
Was a community volunteer,
Led youth and women's groups at church,
Visited the sick whom I held dear.

Now my days stretch out before me;
My daily planner is put away.
Nothing is scribbled under the heading,
"Things that I must do today."

I read the news and work the puzzles;
Then I put the paper away.
I read my Bible and talk on the phone.
Meals with friends highlight my day.

Fortunately, our activity director
Intervenes to save the day,
Redirecting my empty moments,
Keeping restlessness at bay.

## *Diabetes*

Diabetes is a frustrating disease;
No longer can I eat just what I please.
My glucose level dictates what I do,
Even what I can wear – the type of shoe.

Meals have become a time I dread;
If I eat the peas, I must leave the bread.
Desserts must be fresh fruits in a small amount:
Half a banana or seven grapes that I count.

It affects my body from head to toe;
As my feet burn and tingle, I watch my eyesight go.
My aorta is stiff, and wounds slowly heal.
Staying close to a bathroom has become an ordeal.

When blood sugar drops, I'm unsteady on my feet
And must find a high-carb food to eat.
When it rises, lethargy sets in.
Dealing with diabetes, I must fight to win.

## Misplaced Envy

When she was introduced to me,
I envied these things that I could see:
Soft waves all in place define her silvery hair;
Twinkling eyes that picked up the blue she
    chose to wear.
Her smile was warm, inviting, and sincere;
Her daughters with her held her very dear.
There was no evidence that she felt any pain;
She did not use a walker or a cane.

But my envy would quickly disappear
When she said: "Where am I, and how did I get here?"

# *Pain of Separation*

The house is strangely quiet now;
No barks announce a visitor at the door
Or a need to go outside to explore
Or happiness over a family member's return.

No hard nails click across the floor,
Scratch fleas that resist all medication,
Jump upon you with accompanying whines,
Or loudly announce that outside time is over.

No meows suggest it is time to eat,
That a door has accidently closed too soon,
That a bird is perched outside the window pane,
Or that a favorite playmate is not near.

Because I cannot stay, the animals must go.
We were assured the dogs would go to a farm.
And the cats would be placed in loving homes.
But, oh, how I wish that loving home were mine.

It is another penalty of growing old.

## Misplaced Emphasis

The things I snatched in life
And clasped closely to my chest,
God wrested from me one by one:
My pride in parenthood, my femininity,
My independence, my intellect.

Now this empty shell that knows no other master
Finds all that is needed in my Savior's love.

## Changing Our Focus

We have altered the focus of our lives
From providing shelter and food
To seeking out exciting pursuits
That promise to make us feel good.

Entertainment is what we constantly crave,
And we find it on every hand.
The more risqué a movie is,
The more it is in demand.

Electronic devices deliver our mail;
We are seldom away from our phone.
We relish the gossiping news we receive

And stand ready to cast the first stone.

Purity in living is not a concern;
Our idols have no moral worth.
We have lost the standards our mothers knew
And taught us from our birth.

## *Death*

I see your furtive smile
   As you glide silently
      Along the path before me.

I know that somewhere down
   The way you will pause
      And patiently wait for me.

 I cannot elude you forever.

## *Withdrawing Deposits*

I did not know what I was doing
As the years rolled swiftly by;
I was memories accruing
Without thought to when or why.

My perimeters have narrowed now,
And activities are few.
Each day I make it through somehow
By recalling what once I knew.

I think of places I have been
And things the children would say.
I cannot walk that way again,
But I treasure each step of the way.

Each fall I long to go to school;
Daily I miss my church as I pray.
These memories have become a tool
To make my body start the day.

# *To Go or Stay?*

Lord, You must think me quite insane
When I struggle to remain
In a cruel world riddled now with pain,
When I could quickly meet You there
In Your home so bright and fair
Where there is no more sickness, fear, or care.

But I find it hard to leave
Those who would surely grieve
The loss of security, I daily weave.
I can't leave them all alone
Until they can manage on their own,
Yet how long can my departure I postpone?

You know what is best;
My case I rest.